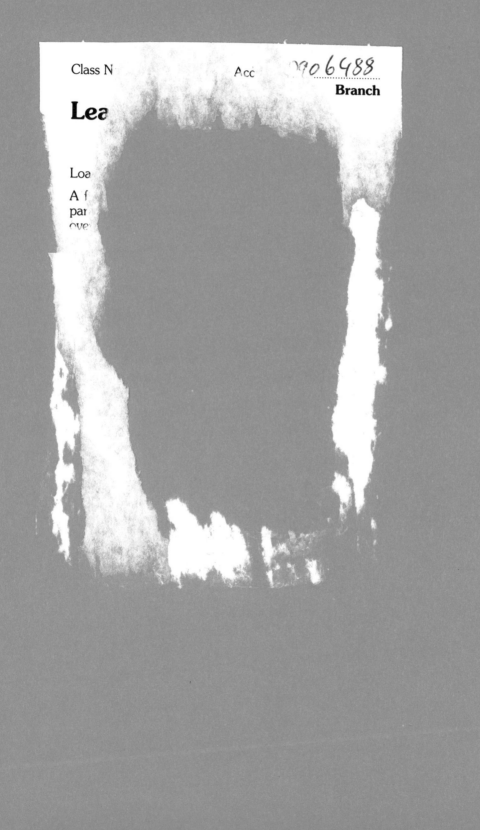

SURFING

Paul Mason

HODDER
Wayland

An imprint of Hodder Children's Books

to the limit

SURFING

Other titles in this well-cool series are:

BLADING

MOTOCROSS

MOUNTAIN BIKING

SKATEBOARDING

SNOWBOARDING

CON

Produced for Hodder Wayland by Roger Coote Publishing,
Gissing's Farm, Fressingfield, Eye, Suffolk IP21 5SH

© Hodder Wayland 2000

Prepared for Hodder Wayland by Mason Editorial Services
Designer: Tim Mayer

Published in 2000 by
Hodder Wayland, an imprint of
Hodder Children's Books

A Catalogue record for this book is available from
the British Library.

ISBN 0 7502 2780 X

Printed and bound in Italy by

Hodder Children's Books
A division of Hodder Headline Ltd
338 Euston Road, London NW1 3BH

WHAT IS

Surfing is the art of riding waves. There are lots of different ways of doing this: on a kneeboard, a body board, using just your body and a set of swim fins, or on an inflatable mat. But most people surf on. . . a surfboard!

SURFING?

Startup Vocabulary Kit

Session	The time from when you paddle out until you ride your last wave into the beach.
"Out there"	Out catching waves; also, not here, on the land.
Gnarly	Difficult, aggressive or, especially, dangerous.
Dude	Another surfer. Be careful with this word: one month it's cool to use it, the next it's not.
Betty	Girl. A surf betty is, of course, a surfer girl.
Out the back	Out beyond the spot where the waves break.
Lineup	Where the waves break, where surfers wait to catch them.
Rights	A wave you turn to the right on.
Lefts	A wave on which you turn left.

Surfing looks simple, but is actually incredibly hard to learn. Once you've learnt, though, you never forget how. There are fifty, sixty and seventy-year-old people surfing today, who learnt back when surfing first became popular. On the same beaches are kids of five or six years old, just catching their first waves: the first of thousands, or tens of thousands, of waves they'll ride in their lifetime.

He'enalu

The Hawaiian word for surfing is *he'enalu*. It comes from two separate words; like many Hawaiian words each has several meanings:

He'e (v.)

1 To ride a surfboard. 2 To flee; to flee through fear.

Nalu (v.)

1 To speak secretly, or to speak to one's self. 2 To think; to search after any truth or fact.

So, surfing is to ride a surfboard; also, perhaps, to flee in fear, and to search for the truth.

Roots

Surfing was born in Hawaii, where riding the best boards, called olos, was only allowed for kings. It first spread to the rest of the world in 1907, when George Freeth came from Hawaii to demonstrate surfing at Redondo Beach in California. But the first famous surfer was Duke Kahanamoku. Duke spread surfing to mainland U.S.A., and to Australia on a visit in 1914.

Five Great Surfing Films

- *The Endless Summer*
- *Big Wednesday*
- *Five Summer Stories*
- *Focus*
- *Kelly Slater In Kolor*

The view from the lifeguard tower at Pipeline, Hawaii. Surfers looked at this break for years before anyone dared to paddle out.

Surfing spreads to Europe

Surfing was brought to Europe by the film industry, but not because people saw surfing at the cinema and wanted to have a go. Instead, two movie-makers working on a film of Ernest Hemingway's novel *The Sun Also Rises* saw the excellent waves of the western French coast near Biarritz. They got hold of some boards and went out to surf: a new sport had arrived in Europe!

Surfers desperate to get to the beach.

Surfing has been around for many years, but first became widely popular in the 1960s. The message was spread by the surf movie. The first movies were made by surfers themselves, but Hollywood soon caught on. Tens of thousands of kids were introduced to surfing by movies like *Muscle Beach Party* and *Gidget*.

Duke Kahanamoku

Duke was not only a great surfer. He was the best swimmer in the world, and won gold medals at the 1912 and 1920 Olympics. He was only finally beaten by Johnny Weismuller, who went on to star as Tarzan in several movies.

Duke himself was also a film star, and played a variety of roles in Hollywood movies. He even acted with another 'Duke', John 'Duke' Wayne, in *The Wake Of the Red Witch*!

Shortboards

Most surfers today ride shortboards. These are slimline performance boards that allow the most radical manoeuvres because of their light weight and speed. They're also much harder to ride than longboards (Malibus) or mini-mals.

Although they look very similar, even slight changes to a shortboard's shape can make it ride very differently. The key elements are length, width, thickness and bottom shape.

Surfboard design variables:

Thick rail

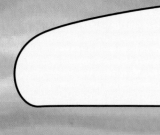

Thin rail

Rail shape

A thick, round rail is easier to control but slower to turn; a hard, thin rail is quicker-turning, but catches in the water if the surfer isn't skilful.

Tail shape

Narrower tails cling to steep waves; wider tails accelerate better but are harder to control.

Nose

A wider nose catches waves better; a narrower nose is easier to ride in steep waves.

Length

Longer, wider boards catch waves better; shorter, narrower ones are easier to turn.

Vee bottom

Bottom shape

Concaves or channels around the fins drive water under the board, making it faster. Vee makes it more manoeuvrable, but more likely to catch in the water and slow down.

Single concave bottom

Favourite Dimensions

One legendary Californian shaper suggests the following dimensions:

Type:	Dimensions:	Bottom shape:
Small wave board	6'0"–6'6" x 19" x $2^3/_8$"	Single to double concave
Larger-wave board	6'8"–7'0" x 18.5" x $2^1/_4$"	Variable vee throughout

Fins

Fins of different sizes make a board go quicker or slower, and affect manoeuvrability.

The Longboard
Revolution

Bonga Perkins surfing at Pipeline, Hawaii.

Definition of a longboard:

Longboards are at least 8'6" long: 'real' longboards are 9' or more. Most are around 9'6", but they can be as long as 12': that's a lot of foam! They have a rounded nose and are fairly thick.

Every year there are more and more longboards in the lineup. Longboards have a lot going for them: they're easy to paddle, they catch lots of waves (even small ones), and they're increasingly manoeuvrable.

Will Eastham, European longboard champion 1999, logs some tip time.

Good things about longboards:

- Catch loads of waves.
- Paddle well.
- Stable and easy to learn on.

And some bad things:

- Often ridden (dangerously) by beginners.
- Greedy riders seem never to give waves away.

Joel Tudor

Joel Tudor was 17 when he first won the World Longboard Championship. He now spends all his time travelling around the world, making appearances for his sponsor and surfing in competitions or for photo shoots.

Who says surfing's hard? Not Joel.

If you're not on a longboard, they can be annoying. You sit there for hours, the perfect wave comes towards you and before it's even broken there's a longboarder on it. This is NOT COOL.

Ridden well, longboards are every bit as exciting as shortboards. They have a fluid style that looks good from the beach and is great fun.

Duane Desoto tuberiding on a longboard.

BASICS AND STYLE

Every surfer in the world has his or her own style. Some are super-cool, hardly seeming to move. Others look like a whirlwind, with arms and legs twisting and turning all over the place.

Whatever your style, it's made up of five basic moves. All the rest are just window dressing.

1 The takeoff

Paddle hard to get the board moving. As it starts to catch the wave, push down on the deck and whip your feet through. Sounds easy. It isn't.

2 The bottom turn

You're on your feet, flying down the face of the wave. To keep going along the wave, instead of in front of it, you need to turn to the side ahead of the white water. Crouching, lean hard into the rail of the board. Only take your weight off the rail as the board comes round.

The top turn

Timing is everything! To avoid flying off the back of the wave, you need to turn back down its face. It's a bottom turn in reverse. Kind of.

The floater

4

A section of the wave crumbles in front of you: turn around the bottom, or float over the top. To pull a floater, hit the top of the wave and keep your board pointing along it. To do this, it has to *feel* as though you're making your board point out of the back of the wave.

The cutback

5

Once in a while, you get too far ahead of the steep, fast bit of the wave. A hard turn back the way you came (and then another one to point you the right way again) is called a cutback.

More style...

Almost all surfing moves are based on the bottom turn, top turn, floater or cutback, but surfers have found more and more variations on these themes. Many surfers also ride skateboards and some go snowboarding: skateboarding, especially, has fed some radical moves into surfing. At beaches around the world you can see kids floating aerials, doing tailslides, reverses, 360s and a load of other seemingly impossible tricks.

New Aerialists

When aerials first appeared in surfing, there was no real attempt to land them and carry on surfing. Now, though, talented young surfers such as Kalani Robb (far left) regularly perform aerials without falling off.

One of the original aerialists, Shane Beschen, continues to push the boundaries of what's possible.

Definitely not stylish:

● Day-glo wetsuits

● Tight, short surf trunks

● Permed hair

● Aggro

● Dropping in (see also Ethics, p.24)

Competition

Most surfers never enter a competition, and there's no rule that says you should. But the best surfers end up competing, because it's almost the only way to make a living as a surfer.

The top surfing competition is the A.S.P. (Association of Surfing Professionals) World Tour. This is made up of the Top 44 surfers in the world, plus others who qualify to compete against them in each event. Feeding into the A.S.P. are qualifying competitions that take place all around the world. In 2000, a new world circuit, the IS Tour, was launched by former pro surfer Derek Hynd.

As well as these competitions there are one-offs like the Eddie Aikau memorial contest, and national and regional contests.

The lefthander at G-land is home to one of the world's biggest – and most remote – surfing contests.

The Eddie

The Quiksilver In Memory Of Eddie Aikau, or 'The Eddie' as surfers call it, is a special competition. You must be invited to enter, and the competition is only held if the waves at Waimea Bay, Hawaii are more than twenty feet high. The competition is held to remember Eddie Aikau, a famous Hawaiian lifeguard and surfer, who died tragically at sea.

WORLD CHAMPIONSHIP TOUR

MONTH	LOCATION	COUNTRY
March	Kirra/Gold Coast	Australia
	Bell's Beach	Australia
April	Manly	Australia
May	Teahupoo	Tahiti
	Torami Beach	Japan
May–June	Tavarua/Namotu	Fiji
July	Jeffrey's Bay	South Africa
July–Aug	Huntington Beach	U.S.A.
Aug	Newquay	England
	Lacanau	France
Sept	Hossegor	France
Oct	Anglet/Mundaka	France/Spain
Dec	Rio de Janeiro	Brazil
	Pipeline, Oahu	Hawaii
	Alii Beach, Oahu	Hawaii
	Sunset Beach, Oahu	Hawaii

A surfer competing at Pipeline, Hawaii, claims big points from the judges.

Greatest Surfer

One afternoon in December, 1995, one surfer won the Chiemsee Pipe Masters, the Hawaiian Triple Crown of Surfing, and his third World Championship. If he'd lost, none of these would have been his. Kelly Slater has since won more world championships, taking his total to six. He is, unquestionably, the Greatest Surfer In The World.

The heat where the world title was won: Slater cheers his friend Rob Machado on.

Slater fact file:

Kelly Slater was born and brought up in Florida, on the East Coast of the U.S.A. He lived twenty minute's drive from Sebastian Inlet, the East Coast's most famous surf spot, and surfed there every day there were waves.

As well as having been a contest machine since he was in high school, Slater has been a T.V. star, in the show *Baywatch*. He has been romantically linked with another of the show's stars, Pamela Anderson, earning him the envy of surfers all round the world!

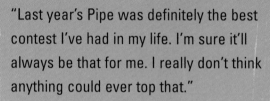

Beach celebrations for another world championship.

Slater on his third world title:

"Last year's Pipe was definitely the best contest I've had in my life. I'm sure it'll always be that for me. I really don't think anything could ever top that."

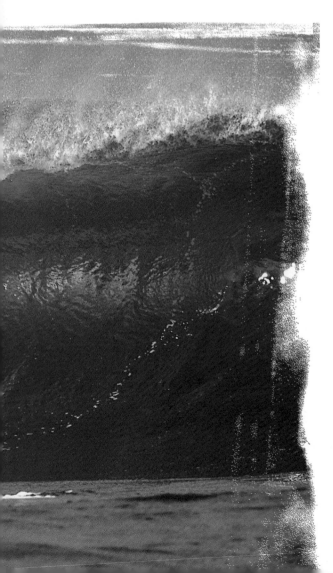

Surf photographers brave the impact zone in the effort to get a picture of the world's best surfer.

HAWAII

Hawaii is at the heart of surfing. It's where the world championship is decided. Every surfer dreams of going to the North Shore for the winter season. This is when some of the biggest waves in the world are ridden. Welcome to Hawaii. . .

Localism

Hawaii is the world's most overrun surfing location, and localism is, understandably, common there. Localism is when surfers from a particular spot try to discourage other people from coming there. At its mildest, it just means local surfers aren't very friendly to visitors. At its strongest it can lead to violence and destruction of surfboards and other property.

Haoles

Hawaiians call non-Hawaiian surfers *haoles.*
The word was first used when white men
arrived in the islands with Captain Cook. It
meant 'without the breath of life, foreigner, or
white man.' As the invasion of Hawaii by white
people following Cook was mirrored by an
invasion of Hawaiian beaches by surfers from
elsewhere, the word began to be used again
to describe them.

. . . land of the super-grommet. . .

Hawaii is where surfing comes from. Duke Kahanamoku spread
surfing out from Hawaii in the 1910s and 1920s, and in the 1950s
Hawaii was where the best American surfers came to test
themselves. It's still the ultimate proving ground.

. . . and the telephoto lens. Well, would you take
water shots in those waves?

Big Waves

For some surfers, the ultimate challenge is to surf in big waves. Surfing is always dangerous, but big-wave surfers risk their lives with every session. In recent years, two of the best surfers in the world, Mark Foo and Todd Chesser, have been killed in big surf.

Big-wave surfers ride larger boards (about 9' long) which help them catch the waves.

Mavericks

One of the most famous big-wave spots is Mavericks' Reef in Half Moon Bay, California. Cold water and currents add to a steep takeoff and dangerous rocks to make this one of the most challenging waves anywhere. It's also part of the Red Triangle – where there are regular attacks on surfers by great white sharks.

Tow-in boards

The ingredients of a tow-in board are as follows:

Heavy, thick glass coat
For strength and to weight the board down.

Lead core
To weight the board down and stop it bouncing off the face of the wave.

Shorter length
Easier to turn. No need for easy paddling.

Footstraps
Keep the surfer's feet attached to the board as it's being towed and while riding huge waves.

Big-wave riders continue to push the boundaries. Tow-in surfing is becoming increasingly popular. Surfers riding specialist boards are towed along by jet skis, to match the speed of giant open-ocean waves (impossible if you're paddling in the normal way). They release the tow line just as the wave is about to break, and ride the wave using natural power.

Laird Hamilton tow-in surfing at Peahi. Laird is 6' tall, so how big is this wave face?

The Largest Wave

Greg Noll, otherwise known as Da Bull, paddled out into giant surf on the North Shore of Oahu, Hawaii and rode down the face of a wave that spectators agreed was at least 40 feet high. He then fell off. No one on the beach thought he could possibly survive, but Da Bull's head appeared in the white water as he swam for shore.

Ethics

Surfers can seem like rebels – it's an image some of them love. But there are rules about how to behave while you're surfing, which are sometimes strictly enforced.

If you think about it, it makes sense to have a set of rules that everyone agrees to. Surfing's dangerous enough as it is: if there was anarchy in the lineup, injuries and accidents would be common.

Crowds in the lineup can equal injuries, so surfers have their own rules about how to behave safely.

Surfing's rules are there to help everyone, and most people are happy to go along with them. But be warned: stories of offenders having the fins punched off their boards, their car windscreen plastered in surf wax, or even worse, are common.

See how the surfers below are checking left and right to see who should ride the wave.

Priority quiz

1 **Five people are all paddling for the same wave. Who gets to ride it?**

a) the surfer with the coolest board;

b) the oldest surfer;

c) the surfer taking off closest to the peak, where the wave first breaks.

2 **You're riding in on the best wave you've caught all day. Someone paddling out is right in your path. What do you do?**

a) start hurling abuse at them and waving them out of the way;

b) try to turn round them;

c) straighten out or turn off the wave, so you're sure you won't hurt them.

3 **You're paddling out and a wave breaks in front of you. There are probably other people paddling out behind. What's the best thing to do?**

a) dump your board and dive as deep as you can. It probably won't hit anyone;

b) check behind you before letting it go;

c) hang on to your board and duck dive or roll it. Even if there's no one behind you, it's good practice.

How did you do?

Mostly a) – you are a complete lame-brain. You shouldn't be allowed outside, let alone out surfing. If you do go out surfing, it won't be long before you're sent back to the beach.

Mostly b) – there is hope: you're not deliberately dangerous, and respect for your elders is a good thing.

Mostly c) – you will be welcome on most beaches, because you're not going to hurt anyone.

Ocean Safety

Imagine someone throwing a bucketful of water at your face, and think how the force of it would push your head back. How many buckets of water do you think there are in even a small wave, and how much damage could they do to your body?

SURFING IS DANGEROUS. Currents, big waves, shallow bottoms, other surfers, rocks – all can catch you out unless you take care. And we haven't even mentioned sharks. . .

Safety tips

● Never surf alone.

● Never surf when there are warning flags out.

● When you fall off, tuck your chin in and, with your forearm in front of your face, wrap one hand over your head. Wrap the other arm round the back of your neck. This keeps your neck from being snapped back and stops your board hitting you in the head.

● Always jump off away from your board, so there's less chance of it hitting you.

● Unless there are rocks in front, it's safest to straighten out in front of the wave and lie down on your board, rather than jumping backwards into the white water.

Currents

If you find yourself caught in a current:

● Don't panic.

● Don't try to paddle against the current. You can never be stronger than the ocean.

● Stay with your board.

● Paddle sideways out of the current. It will continue to sweep you along, but you'll be heading towards the edge, where there will be slower water.

● Once in slower water, head for land.

It's hard to work out if this is worse for the surfer bailing out or the surfers paddling out.

Famous Spots

Canary Islands.

Pretty much anywhere that waves break you can find people trying to ride them. Some spots have been ridden for years; others have only just been discovered; still others are rarely ridden because they're so hard to get to.

Every surfing region has its famous spots. Some kinds of wave are more common in particular places, but generally any area will have a scattering of each kind of wave: reef breaks, beach breaks and point breaks.

Big Sur, California, U.S.A.

Hawaiian reef break.

Point break

Point breaks make waves that roll in along a point of land that sticks out to sea. They break evenly, although sometimes quite slowly, and give excellent long rides.

Two famous examples: Jeffrey's Bay, South Africa; Malibu, U.S.A.

Jeffrey's Bay, South Africa.

Seignosse, western France.

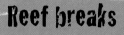

Reef breaks

So called because the waves break over reefs, either close to shore or far out to sea. These waves usually break fast and hard, in shallow water and in a fairly predictable way.

Two famous examples: Pipeline, Hawaii; Uluwatu, Bali.

Balinese reef break, Indonesia.

Bells Beach, Australia.

Beach break

Of course, these break off the beach, on a bottom of either sand or mixed sand and rock. Although not usually as fierce as reef breaks, beach breaks are unpredictable and often hard to surf well.

Two famous examples: Supertubes, Portugal; Bell's Beach, Australia.

The Box, Western Australia.

Glossary

Word:	Means:	Doesn't mean:
Dropping in	Taking off in front of another surfer who has right of way.	Popping by to visit your friends.
Grommet	Young surfer.	Anything to do with DIY.
Ho-dad	Non-surfer; an uncool person.	'Hello, Father!'
Kahuna	Hawaiian royalty; older (much older), respected surfer.	Anything to do with beefburgers.
Localism	Aggression from local surfers aimed at keeping others away.	Pride in your community.
Malibu	Another name for a longboard; also, the Southern California beach where they first became popular.	An alcoholic drink.
Olo	Super-long, super-heavy hardwood board used by old-time *kahunas*.	Hello in Norwegian.
Peak	Place in which the wave first breaks.	Mountain.
Rail	Thin edge of a surfboard.	Thing trains run on.
Rocker	The amount of curve a board has, viewed from the side.	Person dressed in a leather jacket who likes Aerosmith.
Stringer	Thin strip of wood in the middle of a board for strength.	Piece of string.
Taking off	Starting to ride a wave.	Disappearing; running away.
Wahine	Girl or woman.	Exclamation during wipeout.

Books

Fiction:

The Dogs Of Winter Kem Nunn (No Exit Press, 1998), and *Tapping The Source* Kem Nunn (No Exit Press, 1997): two adult but beautifully written novels set in California.

Non-fiction:

Walking On Water Andy Martin (Minerva Press): the musings of a Cambridge professor and surfing enthusiast who finds himself on the North Shore of Hawaii one winter season.

Surfing (Franklin Watts, 1998)

Magazines

There are more surfing magazines than we've got room for here, but a few of the best are *Carve* magazine (U.K. based); *Surfer* and *Surfing* (monthly American magazines); and *Tracks* and *ASL* (both monthly Australian surfing magazines).

Web sites

Again, there are so many that we can't list them all. One of the most useful sites is **www.goan.com/surflink.html**. It's a links site, which offers options of sites all round the world, themed by region. The sites you can go to from goan include surfcams, which have an hourly update of whatever beach they're pointed at; surfshops; travel sites; and surf reports and forecasts.

Index

Picture Acknowledgements
The publishers would like to thank *Carve* magazine for supplying all photos in this title: Pete Frieden 4, 16, 29 (bottom, lower middle); Chris van Lennep 10, 29 (upper middle); Tim McKenna 12 (top), 28 (bottom); Chris Power 18 (top), 19 (top), 29 (top); Mike Searle imprint, 5, 6, 7, 8, 11 (both), 12 (bottom), 13 (all pics), 14, 15 (all pics), 17, 18 (bottom), 19, 20, 21 (both), 22 (both), 24 (both), 26 (both), 27, 28 (top, lower middle); Alex Williams (28 upper middle); Darrell Wong 23.

The artwork on pages 8 and 9 was supplied by Mayer Media.

Weather

Sally Hewitt

Franklin Watts
London • Sydney

An Aladdin Book
© Aladdin Books Ltd 1999
Produced by
Aladdin Books Ltd
28 Percy Street
London W1P OLD

First published in Great Britain
in 1999 by
Franklin Watts Books
96 Leonard Street
London EC2A 4XD

ISBN 0-7496-3431-6

Editor: Jon Richards

Consultant: Helen Taylor

Design

David West • CHILDREN'S BOOK DESIGN

Designer: Simon Morse

Photography: Roger Vlitos

Illustrators: Tony Kenyon, Stuart Squires – SGA
& Mike Atkinson

Printed in Belgium

Contents

Introduction

Hot sunshine, pouring rain, blustery winds and snow are all different kinds of weather. You can have fun learning about the weather.

Find out how the seasons change as the Earth moves around the Sun, and watch out for signs of a storm. Take the temperature, make a wind detector and keep a daily record of the weather where you live.

1 Look out for numbers like this. They will guide you through the step-by-step instructions for the projects and activities, making sure that you do things in the right order.

Further facts
Whenever you see this 'nature spotters' sign, you will find interesting facts and information, such as the different shapes of clouds, to help you understand more about the weather.

Hints and tips

•Put the weather detectors you make where you can reach them safely. Fix them firmly so they don't blow over.

•When you go on a nature walk, take a waterproof coat and a sun hat, and be ready for all kinds of weather. Wear strong shoes and take a bag with a notebook and pencil and something to drink.

•Pay close attention to what is happening in the sky – what clouds you can see, how hot it is, etc...

NEVER LOOK DIRECTLY AT THE SUN!

Wherever you see this sign, ask an adult to help you. Never use sharp tools or go exploring on your own.

Get an adult to help you

This special warning sign indicates where you have to take special care when doing the project. For example, you should never look straight at the Sun. Its powerful rays can damage your eyes and may even cause blindness!

Climate

Some places are hot all year round, whilst others are cold or rainy. The weather a place has all year is called its climate. Make your own mini-climates and see how they affect how plants grow.

Hot, cold, dry and wet

1 Collect four plastic pots, some kitchen paper and a packet of seeds that will grow quickly, such as grass or cress.

2 Put kitchen paper in the bottom of the pots and sprinkle seeds over it. Now put the pots in places to copy different climates.

3 Put one of the pots in the fridge. Here it will be cold, dry and dark, just like a polar climate! Put two pots on a warm, sunny window sill. Only water one of these pots and cover it with a lid.

4 Put the last pot outside, but don't water it. Now see which of these four mini-climates is the best for growing seeds.

All over the world

There are lots of different climates in the world. Which of these match the mini-climates you made?

Temperate climate

Temperate climates have warm summers, cool winters and rain during any part of the year.

Desert climate

It hardly ever rains in a desert climate. Many deserts are very hot, but some, like the North and South Poles, are very cold.

Rainforest

It rains nearly every day in a rainforest, and the air is always damp.

Seasons

The climate in some places can change from being hot in one month to being cold in another. This is a change of seasons. It happens because the Earth is tilted, as you will see from this project.

Tilting Earth

1 You will need a friend and two balls, one for the Sun and one for the Earth. Paint one of them yellow to be the Sun.

2 Paint a line around the middle of the other ball for the equator – an imaginary line around the Earth.

3 Stick matchsticks to the top and bottom for the poles. Now tilt the Earth and you will see that one half is nearer the Sun. It will be summer here.

4 Now walk around the Sun. Watch the half of the Earth that starts off nearer the Sun now become further away. It is now winter in this half.

The seasons

The changing seasons can bring about some dramatic changes to plants and animals.

Spring brings warmer weather after winter. Plants begin to grow and baby animals are born.

Summer is the hottest time of the year. Trees and flowers are in full bloom.

Autumn is colder. Leaves turn brown and start to fall from some trees.

Winter is the coldest season. Animals grow warm winter coats and snow may fall.

During the summer, the arctic hare has a brown coat. In the winter, this changes to a white coat to help the hare hide in the snow.

Wind

The air around the Earth is always moving, sometimes very quickly, causing storms. This moving air is called wind. Build your own detector to measure the strength of the wind.

Wind detector

1 For your wind detector, you will need a long stick, some thin string, tissue paper, writing paper, tin foil, thin card, thick card and a hole puncher.

Get an adult to help you

2 Cut a strip from each piece of paper and foil. Punch a hole in one end of each strip. Tie the strips along the stick, with the lightest at the top and the heaviest at the bottom.

Tissue paper

Writing paper

Tin foil

Thin card

Thick card

3 Take your wind detector outside to see how hard the wind is blowing. A breeze will only move the tissue paper. A strong wind will move the heavier card.

The Beaufort Scale

This scale is used by weather experts to measure the strength of wind.

No wind

Smoke moves

Leaves move

Branches move

Crests in water

Wind whistles

Trees bend

It's hard to walk

Tiles blown off

Trees uprooted

Air pressure

Even though you can't feel it, the air above you presses down on you all the time. This is called air pressure. Changes in air pressure usually bring changes in the weather.

Getting heavy

1 Air pressure is measured using a barometer. To make one, you will need a balloon, a jam jar, a drinking straw, an elastic band, a cocktail stick, scissors and sticky tape.

Get an adult to help you

2 Ask an adult to cut the end off the balloon and stretch it tightly over the opening of the jam jar. Then use the elastic band to hold the balloon firmly in place so that it won't slip off.

3 Tape the cocktail stick to one end of the straw. Tape the other end of the straw to the stretched balloon to make a pointer.

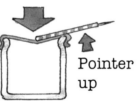

4 Because high pressure brings good weather and low pressure bad, draw the Sun at the top of a rectangle of card and a cloud at the bottom.

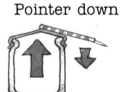

5 Fix the card behind the pointer. Watch your barometer over several days as the changes in air pressure affect the balloon, causing the pointer to rise or fall.

Pointer up

Pointer down

High pressure= Good weather

Low pressure= Bad weather

Barometers

You may have a barometer at home. Its needle shows the air pressure and the kind of weather you can expect.

Compare it with your home-made barometer to see how accurate your home-made one is.

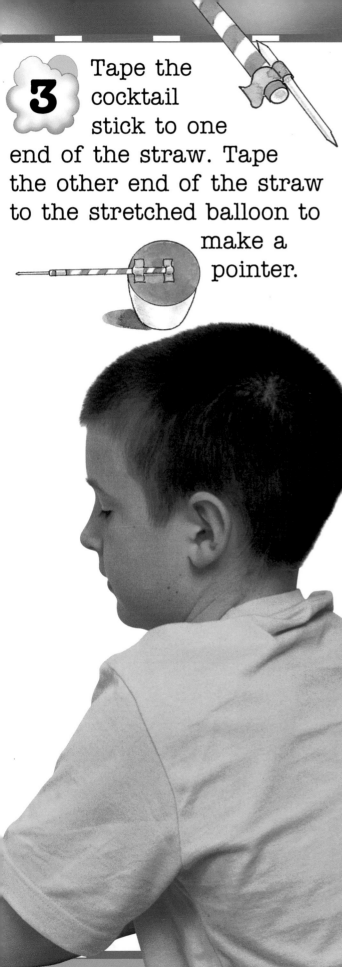

Water vapour

There are tiny droplets of water called water vapour in the air everywhere. Usually, you can't see this water vapour, but when the air cools, this water vapour turns into larger drops of water and forms clouds.

Making clouds

1 You can make a cloud in a bottle. Fill a clear plastic bottle with hot water.

Get an adult to help you

2 Leave the hot water in the bottle for a few seconds. Now pour half of the water away and put an ice cube in the bottle opening.

3 Watch as the ice cube cools the water vapour in the bottle and creates a misty cloud of water droplets.

Clouds

Clouds come in lots of shapes and form at different heights. Their shapes and positions can tell us what weather we will have.

Cirrus clouds are high and wispy. They are a warning of bad weather.

White, fluffy **cumulus** clouds can turn into storm clouds.

Cumulonimbus are dark, towering storm clouds.

Stratus are layers of low clouds and can bring rain or snow.

Falling water

The water and ice particles which make up clouds (see pages 14-15) swirl around and bump into each other, becoming bigger. If they become heavy enough, they fall to the ground as rain, hail or snow.

Collecting rain

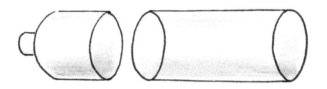

Get an adult to help you

1 Make a rain gauge to see how much rain falls where you live. Cut the top off a clear plastic bottle.

2 Turn the top of the bottle upside down and push it back inside the bottle. Tape over the sharp, cut edges to make them smoother.

3 Put your rain gauge in an open place outside to catch the rain. Prop it up between four bricks to stop it from being blown over.

4 At the same time each day, pour any rain in your gauge into a measuring jug and check how much has fallen.

Snow and hail

Hail is made from ice crystals in the clouds. These clump together to form small balls of ice which fall to the ground.

If it's cold enough, the tiny ice crystals can fall. These are called snowflakes, and each one is different.

Evaporation

When the Sun shines after a rainfall, puddles of water dry out. The water doesn't disappear, it becomes the gas called water vapour (see pages 14-15). When water does this, we call it evaporation.

Drying puddles

1 Fill an old saucer with water and put it on a sunny window sill. Mark the edge of the water with a waterproof marker.

2 Mark the edge of the water in the saucer at the same time each day. The marks will show how quickly the water has evaporated into the air.

The water cycle

The water cycle is the way water moves around between the land, sea and sky.

The Sun heats up the water in oceans, rivers, lakes and puddles and causes it to evaporate.

Water vapour in the air rises and cools. It turns into droplets of water and falls back to the ground. Rivers carry this water back to the sea, where it will evaporate again.

Water rains down

Water evaporates

Water vapour rises

Water flows downhill

Temperature

As the weather changes, you will notice that it gets warmer or colder outside. How hot or cold something is we call the temperature, and you can measure it with a thermometer.

Sun and shade

1 Inside the tube of a thermometer is a liquid. When this liquid heats up, it gets bigger (or expands) and rises up the glass tube.

Get an adult to help you

2 Leave a thermometer in a sunny place. Make a note of the temperature that the liquid inside the thermometer is recording.

BE CAREFUL WITH THERMOMETERS AS THE GLASS CAN BREAK!

Degrees

We measure temperature in degrees Celsius which can be written as °C.

Water boils at 100°C.

100°C

30°C outside feels very hot. Light summer clothes will help you to feel cool.

30°C

Room temperature is 20°C which feels comfortable and warm.

20°C

2°C outside feels cold. You will need to wear a warm coat and hat.

2°C

Water freezes at 0°C.

0°C

3 On the same day, leave a thermometer in a shady place. How does it feel in the shade? Is the temperature higher or lower than in the Sun?

The Sun

The Sun's light and heat are bounced off, or reflected by shiny things. As a result, they can be used to keep things cool. However, dark things take in heat and warm up, as you will see from this project.

Warm and cool

1 You need tin foil, a black plastic bin liner, two thermometers, modelling clay, sticky tape and two clear plastic bottles filled with cold water.

2 Cover one bottle in tin foil and the other with the bin liner. Hold these in place with some sticky tape.

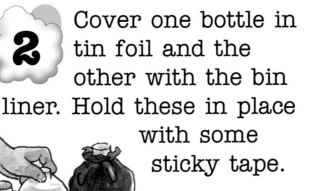

3 Put the thermometers into the bottles and hold them in place with the modelling clay. Put the two bottles in the Sun for about an hour and then check their temperatures. Which bottle is warmer?

Sunglasses

Although the Sun gives us heat and light, its rays are strong and can be harmful.

Sunglasses will protect your eyes from these rays in the summer.

NEVER LOOK DIRECTLY AT THE SUN!

Because snow reflects the Sun, you may even need sunglasses on a bright winter's day!

Storms

Storms are violent forms of weather, with strong winds (see pages 10-11), rain and lightning and thunder. The best place to be during a storm is indoors. But you can still have fun experimenting with storms, even when you're inside.

Thunder and lightning

1 Thunder and lightning happen at the same time. However, because light travels faster than sound, we see the lightning before we hear the thunder. Measure the time between the flash of lightning and the crash of the thunder.

2 It takes three seconds for the sound of thunder to travel 1 km (0.6 miles), so you can work out how far away the storm is. A six second gap means the storm is 2 km (1.2 miles) away.

Whirling winds

Hurricanes are giant whirling storms, hundreds of kilometres across. They build up over warm wet seas and cause a lot of damage along coastal areas.

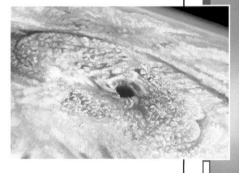

Tornadoes or whirlwinds are spirals of whirling air racing across land. They can pick up trucks, uproot trees and destroy houses in their path.

Pollution

The air around us may look clean but it is full of dirt we can't see. Fumes from traffic, factories and smoke all pollute the air around us, causing nasty weather, such as acid rain and smog.

Smoke gets in your eye

1 This is a way you can see pollution. Cut out a large and a small square of light-coloured cloth – old handkerchiefs will do.

Get an adult to help you

2 Use glue to stick the small square onto the large square of cloth. Glue it lightly as you will need to pull it off later.

3 Hang the cloth up outside nearby, but not on, a busy road.

 4 After at least a week pull the small square away and see how clean the cloth is underneath! Pollution in the air has made the rest of the cloth dirty.

 **Smog and acid rain**
Pollution in the air can make rain as acid as lemon juice! Acid rain damages trees and even wears away stone buildings and statues.

Heavy traffic pumping out exhaust fumes in big cities can cause thick smog, especially on a sunny day. Smog can make it difficult for some people to breathe.

Recording the weather

Use some of the projects in this book to create your own weather station. Keep a note of the measurements and see how they compare them with the weather forecasts in the newspapers or on television.

Keep a daily weather record

1 Hang a thermometer 1.5 m (5 ft) above the ground in the shade. Read it at the same time each day.

Light wind

Light/Medium wind

Medium wind

Medium/ strong wind

Strong wind

2 Your rain gauge will tell you how wet or dry the weather has been.

3 High or low air pressure will help you to tell if the weather is going to be fine or wet.

4 Your wind detector will let you know if it is a good day for flying a kite!

Weather maps

Weather forecasters use little pictures called symbols to make weather maps easy for us to read. Each symbol stands for a certain type of weather.

Dark storm clouds bringing thunder and lightning.

Clouds bringing rain or drizzle.

Clouds broken by patches of sunshine.

Clear skies and sunshine.

The number in the circle shows the temperature in degrees Celsius.

The arrow shows where the wind is coming from and how strong it is.

Glossary

Air pressure

The air around and above you pushes down on you. This is called air pressure. Changes in air pressure usually bring changes in the weather.

Find out how air pressure affects the weather on pages 12-13.

Barometer

This is a device which measures air pressure and can be used to predict the weather.

Build your own barometer on pages 12-13.

Climate

The weather a region has throughout the year is called its climate.

Can you think of different types of climate? Turn to pages 6-7 to see some.

Clouds

Clouds are formed when invisible water vapour in the air cools and turns into visible droplets of water. There are many types of cloud and they are all linked to different types of weather.

Find out how you can make your own cloud and see some different types of cloud shapes and the weather they bring on pages 14-15.

Evaporation

When a puddle of water dries up, the water itself does not disappear – it evaporates. This means that it turns into a gas – water vapour.

You can measure how quickly a puddle of water evaporates in the project on pages 18-19.

Pollution

This can be caused when harmful chemicals are added to the environment. Pollution can cause nasty forms of weather such as acid rain and smog.

The project on pages 26-27 shows you just how dirty the air can be.

Seasons

These are yearly cycles of different types of weather. For example, winter is usually cold while summer is warm.

See what causes the seasons to change throughout the year on pages 8-9.

Storms

These are violent forms of weather, with strong winds and rain.

Turn to pages 24-25 to learn about different types of storm and how you can find out how far away a storm is just by using your watch.

Temperature

This is how warm or cold something is.

Measure the temperature with a thermometer on pages 20-21.

Water vapour

This is the gas form of water. Most of the time it is invisible, but you can see it when the water vapour cools and forms clouds.

See this on pages 14-15.

Wind

Air which moves from one place to another is called wind. Winds can range from a gentle breeze to a tornado.

Measure the wind by building your own wind detector on pages 10-11.

Index

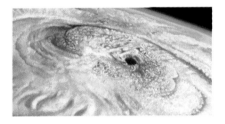